ANY ME
I WANT TO BE

ANY ME
I WANT TO BE

POEMS
by KARLA KUSKIN

9377J

Harper & Row, Publishers
New York, Evanston, San Francisco, London

ANY ME I WANT TO BE
Copyright © 1972 by Karla Kuskin
All rights reserved. Printed in the United States of America.
Harper & Row, Publishers, Inc. Published simultaneously
in Canada by Fitzhenry & Whiteside Limited, Toronto.
Library of Congress Catalog Card Number: 77-105485
Trade Standard Book Number: 06-023615-9
Harpercrest Standard Book Number: 06-023616-7

Once, in a book called THE ROSE ON MY CAKE I wrote a poem that began:

> *If I were a bird,*
> *I would chirp like a bird*
> *With a high little cry.*
> *I would not say a word.*
> *I would sit in my nest*
> *With my head on my chest,*
> *Being a bird.*

It ended with:

> *If I were a sandwich,*
> *I'd sit on a plate*
> *And think of my middle*
> *Until someone ate*
> *Me.*
> *End of the sandwich.*

This became the parent of many similar verses written by children who had read the poem. Their work ranged from "If I were a butterfly" to "If I were a jet plane, I would KILLLLLL."

The idea of being something or someone else is intriguing. Small children have always found an easy identity with animals, especially those that are also small.

> *If you could be small*
> *Would you be a mouse*
> *Or a mouse's child*
> *Or a mouse's house*
> *Or a mouse's house's*
> *Front door key? . . .*
>
> (SQUARE AS A HOUSE)

More and more we encourage children to let their imaginations speak freely. For them, poetry can become the direct route from an emotion to its articulation. In the same way that some stutterers are able to pronounce language smoothly and beautifully when they sing, so many people find that they are able to talk in poetry with a vividness or ease that is not a part of their everyday speech.

The poems in this book are written from the point of view of the subject. Instead of describing how a cat, the moon, or a pair of shoes appear to me, I have tried to get inside each subject and briefly be it.

> *"Who are you?"*
> *Asked the wind.*
> *"I'm the moon,"*
> *Said I.*
> *"And I sit in my spot*
> *Near the top of the sky*
> *With a secretive smile*
> *On my elegant face . . ."*

While one child will think it is ridiculous to imagine being the moon, another may feel it makes more sense than being nine. Hopefully some of those who respond to this idea of trying on different lives will be encouraged to use it and express their own imaginings. It will be rewarding to be in their audience.

Karla Kuskin

ANY ME
I WANT TO BE

1.

I look like you precisely.
You
Clean and combed
Washed well
And dressed up nicely.
But I am paper flat and under glass
Showing you smiling
Standing in your class
While you are jumping up to shout
"That's me!"
Which isn't altogether true.
In fact it's really me you see.
I am a photograph of you.

I do not understand
ARF
How people
ARF
GROWL
BARK
Can walk around on two
ARF
Legs.
I see them in the park
BARK
And all around the town.
They walk around on just two legs
Without
BARK
Falling down!
ARF

PLEASE
KEEP OFF THE GRASS

3.

Stillness is my secret,
Secret stillness.
Sitting in a stream of winter sun,
Sunning on the window radiator.
I'm a cat.
I don't need anyone.

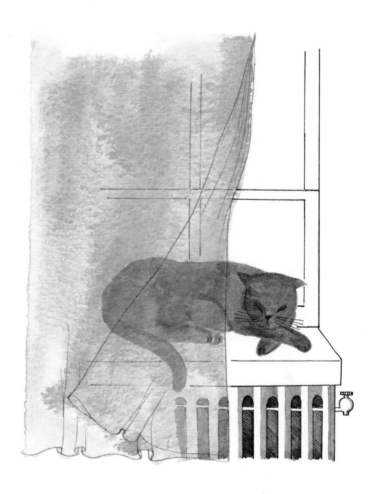

4.

If you,
Like me,
Were made of fur
And sun warmed you,
Like me,
You'd purr.

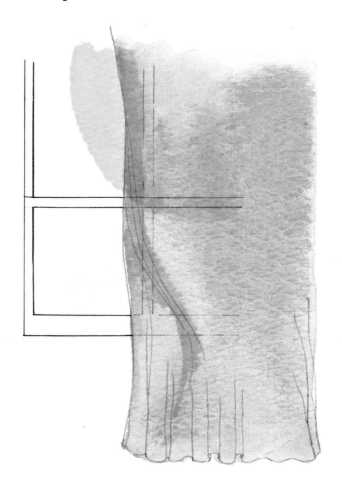

Tick . . . Tock
Tick . . . Tock
ONE
What I do is not too
Interesting
But I suppose it's fun
Tock . . . Tick
Tock . . . Tick
If you want to set the alarm
Pull out the little lever at my back
And you will hear a small click
Tick . . . Tock
Tick . . . Tock
I would tell you who I'm
TWO
And what I do
Tock
But I do not have time
CHIME

6.

True.
We look alike to you;
Green and shaped like hearts.
The wind blows down
And we blow down.
We whisper and get wet
As the rain starts.
But I can clearly see
Each one of us
Is as different
As each one of you.
Some are thinner
Paler
Longer
Tiny.
Patterns differ.
Some are fatter
Greener
Shiny.
Look around my home;
This tree.
You will not find another leaf
Compares to me.

My world is an enormous room
With dust upon the floor.
It sometimes makes me wonder
If there is nothing more to life
Than sweeping dust around a room?
Now if I were a *witch's* broom . . .

I do not laugh or sing or smile or talk.
I cannot count to ten.
My feet don't walk.
My hair is straight
It does not grow or curl,
I do not dance ballet
Or eat a meal
But even so
There is a girl I know
Who thinks I'm real.

My home is a white dome
Under me.
It is very quiet.
My home is a bright dome
Over me.
It is very quiet.
I rest
In my domed home
In the middle of a small sea.
Me.
I am very quiet
Sleeping.
The dome cracks.
The sea leaves.
I wake
Cheeping.

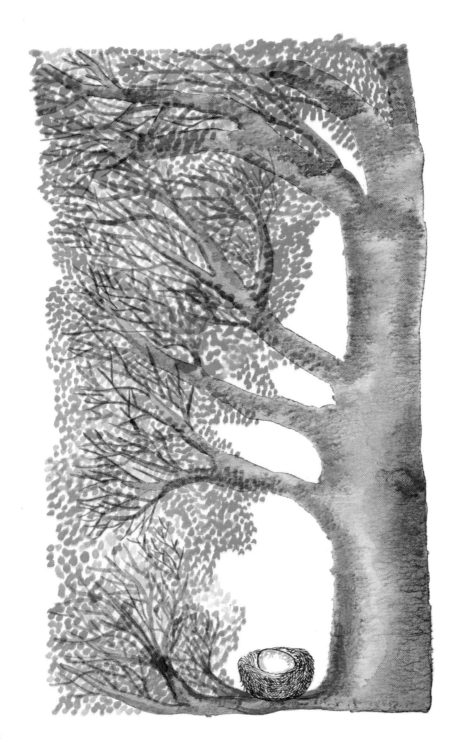

10.

If you stood with your feet in the earth
Up to your ankles in grass
And your arms had leaves running over them
And every once in awhile one of your leafy fingers
Was nudged by a bird flying past,
If the skin that covers you from top to tip
Wasn't skin at all, but bark
And you never moved your feet from their place
In the earth
But stood rooted in that one spot come

Rain

Wind

Snow

Sleet

Thaw

Spring

Summer

Winter

Fall

Blight

Bug

Day

Dark

Then you would be me:

A tree.

If you stood with your feet in the earth
Up to your ankles in grass
And your arms had leaves running over them
And every once in awhile one of your leafy fingers
Was nudged by a bird flying past,
If the skin that covers you from top to tip
Wasn't skin at all, but bark
And you never moved your feet from their place
In the earth
But stood rooted in that one spot come
Rain
Wind
Snow
Sleet
Thaw
Spring
Summer
Winter
Fall
Blight
Bug
Day
Dark
Then you would be me:
A tree.

11.

What there is of me to see
Is short with feathers.
My eyes blink small.
I am not wonderful colors.
I am not tall at all.
I am a puff of dusty grey
Fluffed
Ruffed
Stout.
But sometimes
I open up my small, grey beak
And beautiful songs come out.

Come out and ride around the block with me.
I'll bump a curb.
You bump a knee.
I'll crush fall leaves.
You breathe fall air.
Come out and coast around old trees with me
We're off to anywhere.
My pedals, chains and wheels
Your sneakered feet and socks
Make us fast and free.
Together we can see at least a million blocks.

13.

I'm up here.
You're down there.
And nothing in that space between us
But a mile of air.
Where I sail:
Clouds pass.
Where you run:
Green grass.
Where I float:
Birds sing.
One thin thing there is
That holds us close together:
Kite string.

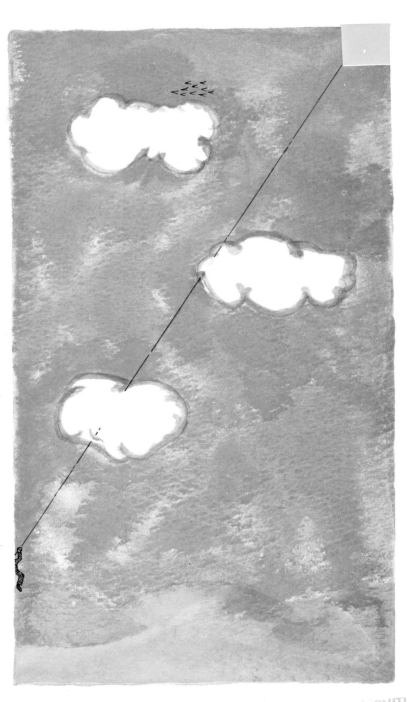

I'm scratched and scuffed.
The socks have holes.
The sidewalk's hard.
I hate the shoves
When boots go on.
One lace is gone.
I sometimes wish that I were gloves.

It's rotten
When there's two of you
Bright red and warm
And then they lose
The other one
And I get wet.
It makes me wish that I were shoes.

16.

I am softer
And colder
And whiter than you.
And I can do something
That you cannot do.
I can make anything
Anything
Beautiful:
Warehouses
Train tracks
An old fence
Cement.
I can make anything
Everything
Beautiful.
What I touch,
Where I blow,
Even a dump filled with garbage
Looks lovely
After I've fallen there.
I am the snow.

17.

When it is dry
I cry.
The rain is a pest and a pain.
When I see flowers
Growing red and high
I hope they will die in their flower bed.
I
Am a sled.

18.

Steel wheels
I have those.
Gears that whrrr and grind in rows.
(No nose.)
Buttons click quick quickly
Lights flashing
Red green green red.
(No head.)
Nuts, bolts, valves, pipes, screws
Fuses
Placed precisely each and every part.
Latches, levers, springs
A thousand metal things
That run as one.
(No heart.)

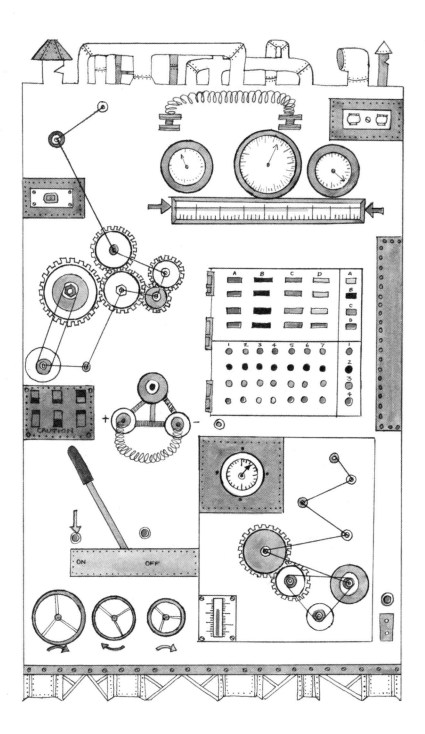

All my legs were very tired.
I had walked, I think, forever
When I came upon a mountain
Wide and high as any mountain
Standing quite alone.
"That's no mountain,"
Said my mother.
"That is just a stone."

We walked on
Me and my mother
Past a dragon that was not
A dragon
But a caterpillar.
Past a very little pot
With some water in the bottom.
"Look," I said, "a lake."
"You are small," my mother told me.
"And you make a small mistake."

All my feet were very weary
I looked up to see the sky
And I saw a tree above me
Tall and leafy
Green and high.
"That's no tree," my mother told me.
"That is just a plant.
It is leafy green and little.
It looks tall
Because you're smaller
Than most things are,"
Said my mother.
Mother is an ant.

I'm swimming around in the sea, see.
And the sea belongs to me, see.
I'm bigger and stronger
Than fifteen
Or twenty
And if you want trouble
Then I'll give you plenty.

A sailboat and a chief of state
Blew by and honked a bit too loud.
Now no one pushes me around
We whales are large and also proud.
I spouted once
And then I ate
The sailboat
And the chief of state.

So
I recommenced swimming
Around in the sea
And spouting about its belonging to me
When a huge ocean liner
Went by at a pace
That left me with ocean all over my face.
I gave a short spout at the shock
And the sound
But I stayed where I was.
As a whale I have found
It is my sea
Until something bigger's around.

Over a stone
Under a fern
Over an aphid
Under an aster
Slight hops
Light hops
Scant hops
Grand hops
Slow hops
Low hops
Long
Strong
Faster.
Flick, snap, gulp, swallow
Beetle, bug and fly
In a wet green bog or hollow
Quicker than an eye can follow
Quicker than a fly can sigh.

I am a creature
That hops on its hands
Sits on its feet
Squats as it stands.
Over and under
Under and over
Beeplant and Bellwort
Creamcups and Clover.
Startings
Partings
Trips and stops
The toad's ways
And the toad's days
Are the ways and days
Of hops.

I am proud.
My head is as green as an apple
And my voice is loud.
When I talk
It comes out in a marvelous squawk.
Everybody jumps.
I crack sweet nuts
And sit
Spitting shells and splitting pits.
When that gets dull
I tear paper into little bits.
Then I split and spit some more
And watch them rush to sweep the floor.
At night
All the funny people come to dinner
Dressed in jewels that clank and shiny leathers
To hide the fact that they do not have feathers.
They gabble, rattle, chitter, chatter
In mouse high squeaks
And low bear growls,

Speaking about something called "war"
And someplace called "Downtown"
And someone called "Mrs."
And what she wore the afternoon they met her.
People's talk sounds boring.
Parrots' talk sounds better.

Squawk.

I liked growing.
That was nice.
The leaves were soft
The sun was hot.
I was warm and red and round
Then someone dropped me in a pot.

Being a strawberry isn't all pleasing.
This morning they put me in ice cream.
I'm freezing.

24.

The night is black
And so am I.
Black and strong I wait
And lie along a branch
To spring and eat
Some soft weak thing
Walking the night black path along
Beneath my feet.
The night is still
And so am I.
Lying in wait
I spring.
A cry.
I have my feast.
The jungle knows the jaguar
And trembles at the beast.

I am a snake.
I snake alone
Through rushes and bushes
Past moss and stone.
I slide through grass,
The slim stalks sigh,
Bees buzz the news
As I slip by.
Mushrooms tremble,
Clover tumbles,
One slight fieldmouse squeaks
And stumbles.
Butterflies and bees and bumbles
Wing away to nests and hives,
Beetles scatter for their lives.
Silence settles where I wend.
The snake is slow to make a friend.

26.

Come picture this lovely and frightening scene;
You're in the river just floating.
You're green.
The sun is so warm on your back
That you smile
And boats filled with people
Speed off for a mile
At the terrible sight
Of your teeth sharp as knives.
Birds vanish like arrows
And call for their wives.
You turn with the breezes
And flick your broad tail
And thousands of fishes
Writhe, quiver and quail.
So if you're a swimmer
Who's fond of a dish
Of low flying feathers
Or tender raw fish,
If people canoeing
Is your kind of meal,
Being a crocodile
Just might appeal to you.

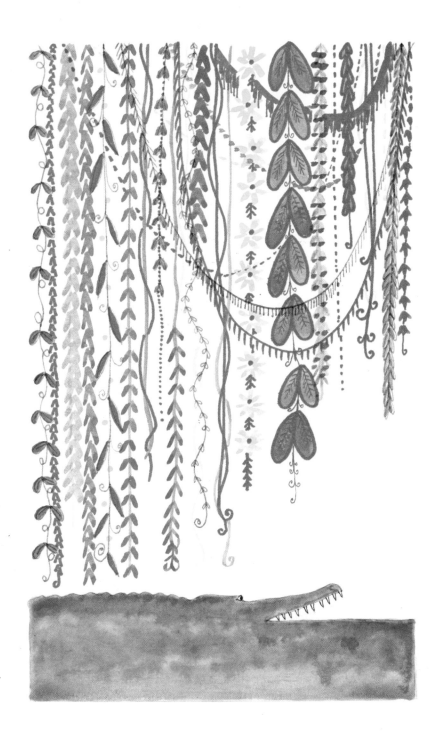

Let me tell you all about me.
Children love me,
You're a child.
All my heads are green and handsome.
All my eyes are red and wild.
All my toes have claws upon them.
All the claws have hooks.
I blow smoke through all my noses.
It is hotter than it looks.
All my tails have points upon them.
All my teeth are sharp and blue.
I won't bite you very badly.
I am fond of you.
All my scales are shaped like arrows.
They will hurt you if you touch.
So, although I know you'll love me,
Do not pet me very much.

28.

One thing that you can say about roaring.
It is not boring.
And if rushing around the jungle being king
Is your kind of thing
You might find the life of a lion
Worth tryin'.

29.

When everything has drawn to a close.
When games are done
And friends are gone from sight
You
And the tired mice
The nesting rabbits
Go to your sleep
As I put out the light.
I'm night.

30.

"Who are you?"
Asked the wind.
"I'm the moon,"
Said I.
"And I sit in my spot
Near the top of the sky
With a secretive smile
On my elegant face
Cold light in my eye
And a pale polished grace.
Glistening
Listening
Just as I've been
Since time was begun.
Watching one star by one
Flicker on
Flicker out
Glowing thin, stouter, stout.
Going stout, thinner, thin
Till I'm only a fine
Brilliant curve of a line
At the end of your sight
In the deep black of night."

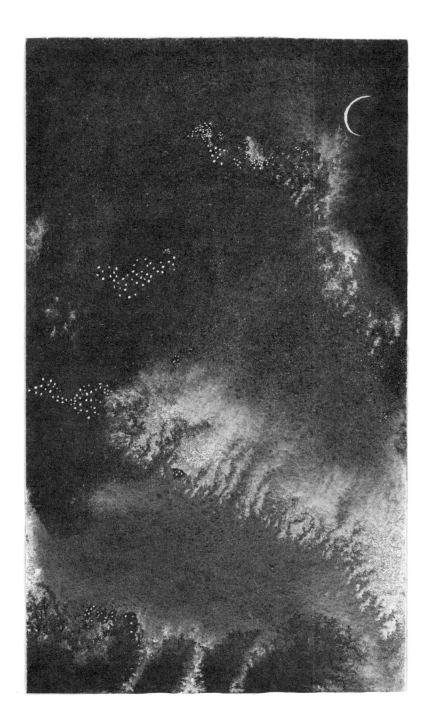

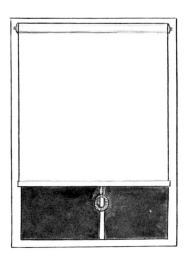

Other Books by Karla Kuskin